TO THE PEOPLE
OF PALMER STATION

CONSULTANT
Dr. William R. Fraser
Polar Oceans Research Group,
Bozeman, Montana.

ANTARCTIC JOURNAL

The Hidden Worlds of Antarctica's Animals

MEREDITH HOOPER

Illustrated by **LUCIA deLEIRIS**

NATIONAL GEOGRAPHIC SOCIETY
WASHINGTON, D.C.

INTRODUCTION

The huge continent of Antarctica sprawls across the bottom of the world—a tenth of all the land surface on our planet. It is weighed down by massive glaciers and permanent ice sheets one to two miles thick. Ice surrounds the continent, growing as sea water freezes each winter, spreading until it covers seven million square miles of ocean. Antarctica is a desert, vast and frozen.

Yet there is life in Antarctica. Abundant, wonderful life. Millions of animals manage to survive in this harsh and beautiful place. The land does not feed them. It is the ocean that fuels Antarctica's life.

Lucia deLeiris and I spent the Antarctic summer in the western Antarctic Peninsula creating this book, living at Palmer Station, an American scientific base on Anvers Island. We observed the animals living on the islands and in the ocean around Palmer, and had many discussions with scientists working there.

Spring begins late in September at Palmer Station. The warmest month is January. Summer slides towards winter at the end of March.

We are grateful to the Antarctic Artists & Writers Program of the United States National Science Foundation for giving us the opportunity to be in Antarctica.

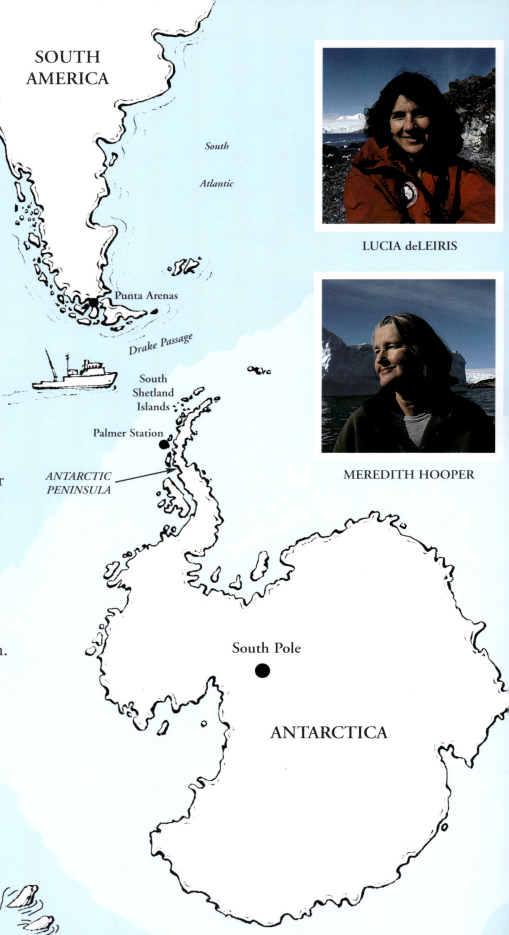

LUCIA deLEIRIS

MEREDITH HOOPER

SOUTH AMERICA

South Atlantic

Punta Arenas

Drake Passage

South Shetland Islands

Palmer Station

ANTARCTIC PENINSULA

South Pole

ANTARCTICA

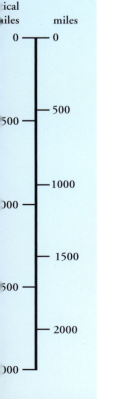

Pack ice at its greatest extent in spring (September, October, and November)

nautical miles   miles
0 — 0

500 — 500

1000 — 1000

1500 — 1500

2000 — 2000

3000 — 3000

A cold autumn wind is twisting the last red leaves off the trees as Lucia and I meet in Boston. For a year and a half we've been planning our Antarctic trip. Now, at last, it has begun.

Twenty-four flying hours later, we step out of a small plane into another cold wind. But the trees here have fresh green leaves. We've come south, 6,500 miles, to Punta Arenas in Chile at the very bottom of South America. And it is spring.

We buy last-minute oranges in the supermarket, send final postcards. But all the time we are thinking about what lies still further over the horizon. South of us, the wide stormy ocean races uninterrupted around the world. South again, Antarctica waits.

A statue of the explorer Ferdinand Magellan stands in a square in the center of Punta Arenas shaded by flowering trees. Lucia and I reach up and touch the foot of an Indian at the base of the statue. Travelers to Antarctica will come back, safely, if they touch the glowing bronze foot. That's the belief.

We are going to Antarctica for three and a half months. There are no trees where we are going. Not even a bush. Our world will be the Southern ocean and small ice-bound islands. It will be a pitching and rolling United States science research vessel, and a scientific base, Palmer Station, on the Antarctic Peninsula.

Our ship, the *Laurence M. Gould*, a sturdy ice-breaker painted bright orange, waits in the harbor.

PALMER STATION

3

The *Laurence M. Gould* wallows and bumps along through heavy seas, laboring up one side of a swell and lumbering down the other. I try to work, my computer lashed to the bench top. Waves slosh past the porthole. Up on deck, getting around is like climbing hills, and the bitter wind almost blows my gloves off. The temperature of the sea has dropped to just below freezing. Silent albatross fly alongside, skimming the surface of the foam-flecked water.

The scientists on board our U.S. science research vessel are here to do geology and study ocean currents. It means much backtracking, being in rough seas, and working around the clock.

Then, at last, we are truly in the ice. At 5:00 in the early morning I go up on deck to brilliant sunshine. There's very little darkness at night now. It's easy to forget about sleep in the Antarctic summer, when it's day most of the night.

We are sailing past magnificent sharp-peaked, ice-clenched mountains. Huge wrinkled glaciers slide slowly to the sea. The edges of the land are walled with cliffs of ice. Penguins bounce through the blue-black water. Minke whales race ahead, backs briefly arching above the surface. Lumps of ice broken off from glaciers and ice cliffs cluster along the shore. A small iceberg drifts by, tilted on its side, water-worn. Adélie penguins balance on its slippery slope, staring at us.

Night comes, but the sun lingers long above the horizon. The sky is green
and golden and the ice glows lemon, with mauve shadows. It's utterly quiet.
A crabeater seal rests on a floe, where the ice lies thick against the land. Her pup
was born in early spring on an icefloe like this. Now she is alone again. Home is
always the ocean or an icefloe for crabeater seals.

The *Gould* pushes and shoves through pack ice. Big blocks of ice rear up, tip, and turn upside-down. Underneath the ice is stained a rich golden brown. The water between is brown as slushy soup.

This is it! The Antarctic meal table.

Staining the ice are minute plants. All winter they've lived on the underside of the ice in tiny holes and hollows. Now, as Antarctica warms, the floes break up and begin melting. The plants, mostly diatoms, are released into the sea in a golden brown mush.

Lucia and I lean over the side of the ship as samples of ice are hauled up for us in a net. A frozen krill comes on board stuck to a small ice lump. All winter young krill live under the sea ice, paddling their ten legs to stay afloat, munching plants off the floors of ice hollows. This little krill is an inch long. Lucia puts it under the microscope and we see its bulging black eyes. A last meal of diatoms lies like a greeny-yellow ball in its transparent body.

Around us the water churns, distributing food for all the different kinds of plants drifting and floating within it. Each microscopic single-celled plant is smaller than the width of a hair. But each is grabbing energy from the sun and nutrients from the water to help make another version of itself, and another, and another. The plants will reproduce in their billions in the brief weeks of summer, floating in great patches, or blooms.

Everything that lives in Antarctica, from the largest whales to the smallest fish larvae, depends on the tiny plants hidden in the ocean.

I stare down into the blue-black depths, trying to imagine all the microscopic plants. Without them and their rich burst of summer growing, nothing can survive.

Lucia puts slices of brown-stained ice under a microscope in the ship's laboratory. We peer at the little diatoms. But all we can see are small browny yellow dots, and strings of dots in a chain. Lucia needs images from much more powerful microscopes to paint what they really look like.

A zoo of animals lives in the ocean grazing on the ocean's tiny plants, spinning and looping through the water, darting, pulsing, floating, drifting. Transparent microscopic creatures eating, and being eaten. Armored copepods moving purposefully in small jumpy skips. Swarms of barrel-shaped blue-tinged salps, stuck together in floating chains. Minute creatures with red eyes, sliding through the water in a curving path like a ribbon.

But most important of all are the ever swimming, ever watchful, two-inch-long Antarctic krill. Now it's summer and krill travel through the wide ocean in great swarms or schools seeking the places where billions of tiny plants collect.

Krill can live to be more than five years old. But many never get the chance. Almost everything in Antarctica of any size eats krill, or eats something that eats krill.

Up on the bridge of the *Gould*, it is just possible to see, through binoculars, the aerials of Palmer Station on a distant headland. But we can't get through. The pack ice is too thick. We have to turn away.

11

All winter bitter winds buffeted the great glacier at Palmer Station, and swooped down the ice cliffs. Snow fell, silently, blanketing the rocky islands in the bay. The days were dim and the nights long.

With spring, water began dripping from winter-deep drifts. The sea ice cracked and shifted, but the small islands scattered through the bay were still frozen white humps. A Weddell seal gave birth to her pup on the ice by the frozen blue walls of the glacier— the first seal pup of spring. Its soft wrinkly fur coat seemed too big for its new body.

But now Antarctica's summer clock is running. And our ship has finally got through to Palmer.

The islands are tumbled rocks scraped bare, streaked with snow. Just behind the blue-painted station buildings, the glacier stretches its slowly melting fingers between heaps of boulders and gravel. Lucia and I walk up to look at the glacier. We have to sign out when we go to the "backyard" and sign in on return. It's safer to know where everyone is.

Two elephant seals come heaving out of
the sea, pulling forward, heads up with the effort.
They scratch their skin with their nails as if they
have hands trapped inside their short flippers.
They take no notice of us at all.

Elephant seals swam to the islands in spring,
as soon as the sea ice began to break up, looking for bare
beaches. The huge bulls fought, and their throaty roars vibrated
across the bay. The females gave birth to pups on the pebbles.
Now elephant seals lie around on any rocks they please,
head to tail, flippers over each other, making comfortable
rattly rumbles and gurgles, sneezings and mutterings.

13

Animals seek out precious bare ground in Antarctica. They need nest sites, and places to rest, and molt, and raise their young. At Palmer animals share the rocky promontory and its buildings with humans. There are 38 of us living on the station. But the islands belong to the animals.

Every day scientists at Palmer go out to the islands to work. Lucia and I have special permission to visit islands. But we have to pass our boating tests, and learn to use the Zodiacs, the flat-bottomed rubber boats tied up in a row by the rocks.

Matt and Pete, the bird researchers, take us with them to help count penguins and occupied nests. We pull on red survival suits and heavy boots, strap on life-jackets, and set off in the Zodiac through chips of ice slishing along the shore, past a small iceberg. I look hopefully at a sloping pebbly beach as we approach Dream Island. But no—we tie up at high rocks and scramble and climb. The beaches are for the penguins.

Adélie penguins build their nests in the same place every year, carrying pebbles carefully in their beaks. We help with the counting, repeating the count three times, then working out the average. It's like counting a crowd at a railway station.

Next day, nest-counting on Christine Island, I watch penguins coming ashore, flicking quickly through the waves, jumping onto the rocks, balancing carefully on their pink feet, climbing up to the higher safer rocks where their mates wait on their nests.

But it begins to snow. Weather can change very fast at Palmer and we head home. Sealed blue drums with emergency tents, food, and sleeping bags are kept on some islands. In the comfort of the boating shed, Ross, who is in charge of boats, has taught us how to put up the tents and use the stove. Very different from a freezing rocky island in a gale.

The sea is choppy and we are wet and cold. I think of the snow settling on the penguins in their pebble nests. We humans survive here in Antarctica because we bring everything we need from the outside world. Getting back to the warm station, a hot drink, and Dawn's fresh-baked cookies is wonderful.

Cormorant Island looks as if it's made of cream-colored cement with rocks stuck in.

But it's quiet to walk on, and the cement is soft as putty because it's guano, from the droppings of blue-eyed shags.

A few blue-eyed shags still sit tall on their tall round nests, built high on the highest rocks. The wind blows, and they face into the cold. The nests are old, made of seaweed and mosses woven through the cream-colored guano like thick brown wool. Blue-eyed shags use the same nesting sites year after year. But most of the nests, filled for so long with the next generation of chicks, stand empty, like dilapidated houses.

Lucia and I scramble up to the top of a cliff and stand in the biting wind looking at the nests. The birds ignore us. They don't move. They make no noise. Some of the nests have two or three big floppy chicks crammed into them, untidy heaps of gray down. The tall thin adult can't cover the chicks, and they spill out over the sides.

I'm writing notes with bare fingers, Lucia has taken a glove off to sketch. It's bitterly cold. Matt and Pete arrive and walk quickly among the nests counting chicks. The parents move their necks sinuously, like snakes, and grunt warnings. Bigger chicks struggle to their feet, copying the adults.

A shag flies in and stands on the edge of its nest. The oldest chick clambers upright and starts pecking, pecking at the base of the parent's beak until it opens. The chick's head goes in, almost disappearing like an arm inside a sleeve. The meal moves from parent to chick with heavy plunging movements.

But afterwards the chick goes on calling with high grunts, and urgent, frantic squawks. It's still hungry.

The number of blue-eyed shags on Cormorant Island has drastically declined. On the way back to the station we pass over the huge upturned hull of a sunken Argentinian ship. A sheen of oil still lies across the sea.

The blue-eyed shags fish in shallow local waters, diving for many kinds of fish. They never fly far from land. The scientists think that oil spills from the wreck affected them badly.

In the wet lab little transparent krill swim around and around in a tank. Lucia studies them. Drawings tend to be of dead krill. Lucia wants to capture what they look like alive and swimming.

Doug, an underwater cameraman, is here to film the krill in the ocean. They swim 100 feet down, he says, in a band three feet thick. If you look up from below, their black mass blocks the light. Sometimes krill collect in an enormous writhing ball. The krill push and squirm into the center of the ball because it's the safest place to be.

Doug says krill can swim faster than he can, but he doesn't know how long they can keep up the speed. He puts his finger into the tank and shows me how a krill moves away fast, defensively, with a rapid jerk.

But their defenses aren't much help when southern humpback whales arrive one morning. The humpbacks lunge through the middle of a seething mass of krill, mouths wide open, gulping. Or they swim in a circle blowing bubbles of air, which trap the krill, like a net.

One is a large male with a kink on his right tail fluke. In a day he can eat two million krill. This summer's feeding in Antarctica must last the humpbacks until they come south again next summer.

In the evening we go out in the Zodiacs. Two humpbacks are cruising together slowly, relaxed. The water shines with a silvery sheen as if satin has been poured over its surface. Bits of brash ice float in the satin. We never know where the humpbacks will appear next, so we listen for the sudden heavy sound as they blow. First the small dorsal fin appears, then the high curving arch of the back. Sometimes they lift their great heads or raise the flukes of their tails. Suddenly both whales are coming straight towards us. One swims directly underneath our Zodiac. I kneel in the bottom and lean over the side as the solid dark gray back, the enormous flippers, the white mottling on the body, passes on and on beneath. Forty feet of humpback whale, just below me in the freezing Antarctic water. Humpbacks in their element.

The sun shines brilliantly. It's the middle of summer and so warm the penguins are panting. The temperature is just below freezing.

The first Adélie chicks pecked their way out of their eggs three weeks ago, early in December. Now they lie on their stomachs, feet sticking out behind, cheeping high small cheeps. Most nests have two gray fluffy chicks, hatched three days apart. One parent guards the chicks while the other searches in the sea for krill.

I watch a shiny clean penguin come jumping up the rocks from the sea, hurrying back to its nest. It weaves through the colony, avoiding pecks. It finds its mate and both birds greet, standing close together, waving their heads and raising their beaks in loud cries. The oldest, strongest chick reaches up and pecks frantically at the newly arrived parent's beak until it opens. The chick pokes its head inside and gulps a meal of half-digested krill. The smaller chick wobbles up for its turn. Both chicks, their stomachs full like little bulging sacks, flop back down into the nest.

Now the grubby, thirsty, hungry penguin can leave nest duty. It hurries to a snowdrift to eat snow. I track it as it patters on little pink feet down the rocks to the beach. A group of penguins stand by the water, waiting, checking for danger. Then, all together, they rush in and swim out to sea. The penguin I've been watching will be away for up to a day, finding food.

I'm sitting on a rock holding a chick in my arms. Its white down is the lightest, finest thing I've ever felt. Deep inside the down the body radiates warmth. Its little bright eyes gaze solemnly above a strong pink bill. Its feet are gray and webbed and soft. It's the size of a small turkey.

The chick's parents walk around my boots. If they stretched out their wings they would measure over six feet from tip to tip. These are giant petrels, and their massive bills can pierce the skin of a whale. But they aren't taking any notice of me. The male is busy poking at a notebook, and the female is fussing over a glove. Donna, who studies giant petrels, kneels down feeling in the feathers on the female's back for the tiny satellite transmitter she put there yesterday. She adjusts the short aerial. We put the chick back in its nest. All around, giant petrels are sitting in rock nests on sharp rock ridges, gazing out unmoving over wide island views to the sky and the sea.

Giant petrels are scavengers, flying across oceans, checking the surface of water and ice for the dead and the no longer needed. They also eat krill, squid, and young penguins. But now they have come onto land, to lay their egg and raise their chick.

Giant petrels can aim a stream of foul-smelling sticky stomach oil at an intruder from a distance of two or three yards. But the giant petrels on the islands around Palmer Station have gotten used to Donna. So she is learning things about their lives no one knew before:

How the female can fly 1,400 miles in five days on one feeding trip away from the nest. How young inexperienced birds build nests of moss, which are soft, but stay damp, while older birds build nests of hard stones, which drain well, much better for the chick. How three months after fledging, this soft chick I've just been holding will be flying as far away as New Zealand, Australia, Argentina, Chile, searching for its own food.

On Humble Island elephant seals rear up and shove their chests against each other, with loud slow rumbling roars. They are young males, practicing fighting. They gape their pink mouths wide, glaring with large bloodshot brown eyes. Groups of elephant seals lie packed together in strong-smelling puddles of their own making, yawning, dozing. They are molting and small bits of skin and hair flake off. Their hides look like old carpets.

Every now and then an elephant seal flops along to the water and swims away to feed. They can dive deeper than most whales, down to the darkest depths, to hunt fast-swimming squid.

Sometimes elephant seals heave too close to the Adélie penguins' nests. I watch the penguins jig from foot to foot uneasily and squawk. Elephant seals can crush and destroy a nest without noticing. They started arriving at these islands in large numbers about 20 years ago. They like using the same spaces as the penguins.

Chinstrap penguins have begun using the islands to nest. At first single birds came, but now there are enough chinstraps to move into Adélie colonies and begin raising chicks.

A few gentoo penguins have arrived as well. The white patch above their eyes looks like a drift of snow. Their felty feet are the same red color as their beaks. Heavy birds, they stand around, squawking.

All summer South Polar skuas have been splashing in a meltwater pool in the backyard. There are 30 or 40 of them, mostly nonbreeders. Now, suddenly, one decides I'm on its territory. It wheels high then swoops, diving for my head, getting between the sun and me so I'm dazzled. I duck, but it wheels around again, and ranges in lower, crying with a high-pitched mewling sound, big webbed feet and claws out like landing gear. I move away fast, until I'm off its space.

Brown skuas are here on the islands as well, nesting high on lookout rocks, ever watchful. They swoop aggressively if anything comes too close to their nests. Brown skuas can eat fish, krill, and the eggs and chicks of blue-eyed shags, but their main summer food comes from penguins. Early in the summer they take unguarded eggs. Now they watch for wandering chicks.

Two leopard seals float into our harbor on a small high floe.

They are here for the hunting. We go past quietly in the Zodiac and I look ten feet of top Antarctic predator in the eye. Leopards eat fish, krill, and young crabeater seals. Now they will eat penguins.

The leopard seals watch us boldly, alert. Their wraparound smiles hide sharp teeth and huge gaping jaws. Their large snakelike heads, on sinuous bodies, swivel to get a good view. Next morning a Zodiac has deflated, its pointy end chewed by a leopard seal.

It's late in the summer. Fur seals arrive, young males slithering up out of the sea, climbing all over the islands.

The Adélie penguin chicks are big and very hungry. Their need for food is so urgent both parents are out in the sea foraging for krill. Some chicks have new feathers showing under their browny gray down, which hangs on in ragged clumps. Others are still covered in gray fluff. They lie in groups, cheeping, or trudge along trying out throaty half-adult greeting noises.

The adults will leave during the next three weeks. The pebble nests are trampled flat; the ground is stained red with droppings. Dust and feathers rise from the bigger colonies. Skuas fly over, in wide low sweeps, or strut boldly among the chicks. A penguin comes in from the sea, clicking over the pebbles, and calls her chicks. But she does not feed them. Instead she backs off, then runs away, fast. The chicks chase her across the rocks, heaving along, stumbling, tumbling over. They have to persist to get a meal now.

At some point the parents just don't come back. The chicks start using up their reserves. They get hungry. Little groups of newly fledged chicks go down to the beach. They are thin and small looking, with blue-black feathers, and no white ring yet around their eyes. They stand looking at the sea. They have never been in the water. Never swum. Never caught a krill. All at once they scramble into the waves, bobbing about on the surface like corks. They try putting their heads under, and bob up again. They have to learn to swim, fast. Giant petrels float in the water. Leopard seals wait, "picking them off like popcorn," says Bill the penguin scientist. Everything is out to eat them.

Suddenly the chicks dive down and start swimming. They have become penguins. The ocean is now their home.

Summer is almost over. Darkness fills the night sky. Soon the surface of the sea will begin to freeze. Bitter storms will shrivel the life out of any summer animals staying too long. Snow starts drifting over the bare stones, the brown boulders, the clanking pebbly beaches. The sharp outlines of the islands blur.

On the station the Zodiacs are brought into the boat house. People are leaving. The station begins to settle down into the winter routine.

Lucia and I have said our goodbyes. The *Laurence M. Gould* arrives and we find our cabins. On the way back, Drake Passage is as rough as usual. In Punta Arenas we return our Antarctic clothing to the depot. Then we head north. To spring, and home.

But down inside the sea, under the newly forming lid of ice, it is warmer than the harsh world above. And calm.

Here there are always living things. The life that makes all other lives possible.

ANTARCTIC ANIMALS, SEA ICE, AND CLIMATE WARMING

Every winter the sea around Antarctica freezes. Enormous awe-inspiring stretches of ice cover the surface of the ocean, heaped-up, flat, wrinkled, thick, thin, glittering white. In spring the ice begins to crack and rot. By the end of summer much of the sea ice has broken up and melted.

The amount of sea ice that forms each year, the timing of its growth, then shrinking, affects the way that everything in Antarctica lives and gets its food, from the tiniest zooplankton to the mightiest whales. The ocean's microscopic plants grow and spread with the breaking up of the ice.

The way animals feed, travel, grow, and breed relates to the presence or absence of ice. The behavior of the sea ice is of vital importance to Antarctica and all that strives to survive here at the bottom of the world.

The animals in this book all live on islands near Palmer Station and in the surrounding ocean. But important changes are happening in this part of the western Antarctic Peninsula. During the last 50 years the winters have become much warmer. Warmer on average by eight degrees F. The summers are heating up. Warmer temperatures have meant less sea ice. This suits animals that live farther north, and they are moving south. Elephant seals now breed around Palmer. Chinstrap penguins have begun nesting, and gentoos are present in large numbers. More and more fur seals swim in. But Adélie penguins and Weddell and crabeater seals depend on sea ice. So do krill. Scientists are finding that the big Adélie penguin colonies are shrinking in this important transition area, and Weddell and crabeater seal numbers are declining.

Less sea ice also means more evaporation, so more snow, which restricts the amount of land free for animals. Snow increases the problems for nesting birds, especially Adélie penguins. So Palmer Station and its islands are particularly interesting to scientists studying how changing climate affects the ecosystem, and how all living things depend on each other, and affect each other.

THE ANTARCTIC FOOD WEB

Not many large meat-eating predators live in Antarctica. Predators eat animals that live on other animals which eat plants, or they eat animals that eat plants. This means that meat-eaters need a lot of space. Their space has to support the animals they eat, as well as the plants that those animals eat. In Antarctica all the plants are microscopic, and they grow in the ocean and in the ice. Made of tiny single cells, they float near the surface where they can absorb sunlight during the few bright months of spring and summer.

Scientists study the Antarctic food web. Although it is not simple it has some simple, clear, short stages. The largest animal on earth, the blue whale, eats the two-inch-long krill. Krill graze on the ocean's microscopic plants – each krill eats a billion plants in its lifetime. The powerful leopard seals eat young crabeater seals, penguins and krill. Crabeaters and penguins eat krill. Krill eat plants.

All life in Antarctica is linked and bound within the food web. All life is sustained by the tiny plants of the sea.

INDEX

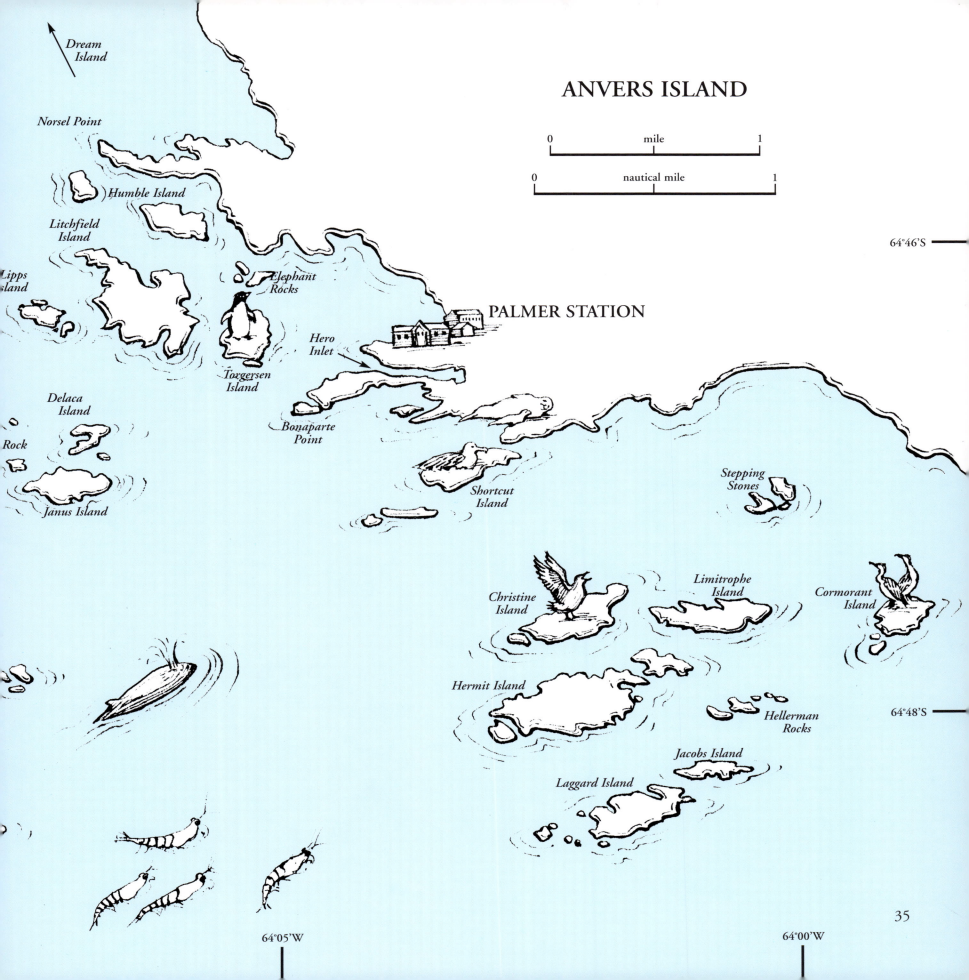

ANVERS ISLAND

Dream
Island

Norsel Point

Humble Island

Litchfield
Island

Lipps
Island

Elephant
Rocks

Torgersen
Island

Hero
Inlet

PALMER STATION

Delaca
Island

Rock

Bonaparte
Point

Janus Island

Shortcut
Island

Stepping
Stones

Christine
Island

Limitrophe
Island

Cormorant
Island

Hermit Island

Hellerman
Rocks

Jacobs Island

Laggard Island

0   mile   1

0   nautical mile   1

64°46'S

64°48'S

64°05'W

64°00'W

35

ACKNOWLEDGMENTS

Being able to live and work in Antarctica
is a very great privilege. We are grateful
to the Antarctic Artists & Writers Program of the
United States National Science Foundation
for giving us the opportunity to be there.

Published by the National Geographic Society
1145 17th Street N.W.
Washington, D.C. 20036-4688

The Society is supported through membership dues and income
from the sale of its educational products.
For more information, please call 1-800-NGS-LINE(647-5463)
or visit the Society's website at: www.nationalgeographic.com

Library of Congress cataloging-in-Publication Data
Hooper, Meredith.
    Antarctic Journal/by Meredith Hooper; illustrated by Lucia deLeiris.
    p. cm.
ISBN: 0-7922-7188-2 (hc.)
    1. Zoology —Antarctica—Juvenile literature.
    2. Summer —Antarctica—Juvenile literature. [1. Zoology—Antarctica.
    2. Summer –Antarctica. 3. Antarctica.] 1. DeLeiris, Lucia, Ill. 11. Title.
QL 106 .H65 2000
591.998'9—dc21   00-035496

Set in Garamond

Printed in Hong Kong

First published in Great Britain in 2000
by Frances Lincoln Limited,
4 Torriano Mews, Torriano Avenue, London NW5 2RZ

1 3 5 7 9 10 8 6 4 2